THE FUNNIEST MAN CITY QUOTES... EVER!

Also available

The Funniest England Quotes... Ever!

The Funniest Liverpool Quotes... Ever!

The Funniest Chelsea Quotes... Ever!

The Funniest West Ham Quotes... Ever!

The Funniest Spurs Quotes... Ever!

The Funniest Arsenal Quotes... Ever!

The Funniest Newcastle Quotes... Ever!

The Funniest United Quotes... Ever!

The Funniest Leeds Quotes... Ever!

The Funniest Boro Quotes... Ever!

The Funniest Forest Quotes... Ever!

The Funniest Sunderland Quotes... Ever!

The Funniest Leicester Quotes... Ever!

The Funniest Saints Quotes... Ever!

The Funniest Everton Quotes... Ever!

The Funniest Villa Quotes... Ever!

The Funniest QPR Quotes... Ever!

The Funniest Celtic Quotes... Ever!

The Funniest Rangers Quotes... Ever!

THE FUNNIEST MAN CITY QUOTES... EVER!

by Gordon Law

Copyright © 2017 by Eagle Books.

No part of this publication may be reproduced, stored in a retrieval system or transmitted in any form by any means, electronic, mechanical, photocopying, or otherwise, without prior written permission of the publisher Eagle Books.

contact@gmediagroup.co.uk

Printed in the USA and Europe
ISBN: 978-1-917744-27-0
Imprint: Eagle Books

Photos courtesy of: Kostas Koutsaftikis/Shutterstock.com, Photo Works/Shutterstock.com, Vlad1988/Shutterstock.com.

Contents

Can You Manage?..9

Boardroom Banter...23

Best of Enemies..29

Managing Players...41

Lifestyle Choice..55

A Funny Old Game.......................................67

Call the Manager..83

Talking Balls...97

Reffing Hell...119

Say That Again?...125

Introduction

The legendary Malcolm Allison may be known as one of football's finest coaches – but his flamboyant personality made him one of the most entertaining too.

Big Mal's coaching brilliance was matched by an endless supply of hilarious remarks and controversial opinions during his tenure with Manchester City.

Mario Balotelli is another playboy character who is equally engaging off the pitch as he is on it, with his bizarre behaviour and fashion sense, and incredibly bonkers statements.

His public spats with manager Roberto Mancini during their love-hate relationship were always enthralling, while Mancini also had a constant war of words with Carlos Tevez.

Tevez – along with Emmanuel Adebayor – was never afraid to fire back at Mancini's criticism, much to everyone's amusement.

The king of gibberish must be Kevin Keegan, who has produced a string of bone-headed quotes down the years. He's among the many City names who have had fans in stitches with their strange sound bites.

There have been comic rants from Joey Barton and Craig Bellamy, funny one-liners from Mike Summerbee and Francis Lee, and who can forget the Scouse wit of Joe Royle?

Many of their classic quips can be found in this unique collection and I hope you laugh as much reading this book as I did in compiling it.

Gordon Law

THE FUNNIEST MAN CITY QUOTES... EVER!

CAN YOU MANAGE?

THE FUNNIEST MAN CITY QUOTES... EVER!

"Management is the only job in the world where everyone knows better. I would never tell a plumber, a lawyer or a journalist how to do his job but they all know better than me every Saturday."
Joe Royle

"You're not a real manager unless you've been sacked."
Malcolm Allison

"The nickname 'Bobby Manc'? Yes, I like it a lot!"
Roberto Mancini on the moniker given to him by the fans

Can You Manage?

"As I said to Kevin Horlock, we can't all be generals, someone has to stand on the pavement and wave as the generals go by on their horses, and if there is no one there, the generals wouldn't go by on their horses."
Kevin Keegan

"I'm thinking of taking a window cleaner's job to fill the spare hour in the evening."
Stuart Pearce says he has plenty of time to juggle the England U21 job with his role at Manchester City

"I may be a Scouser but I'm not stupid."
Joe Royle

THE FUNNIEST MAN CITY QUOTES... EVER!

"Before the match my daughter said, 'Beanie the horse wants to sit next to you by the drinks holder on the touchline'. It is difficult to tell a seven-year-old, 'This is the Premiership, I'm known as Psycho and I'm a hard man'."
Stuart Pearce

"I am a scientist. My training is brilliant and, like all scientists, I can make things work."
Malcolm Allison

"I may have been the captain when we went down but not when we hit the iceberg."
Joe Royle

Can You Manage?

"Fergie's very supportive and understanding with fellow managers. Unless you beat him."
Frank Clark on Sir Alex Ferguson

"If I was waving my hands, then it can happen sometimes. If it upsets people, I will try not to do it again next time."
Roberto Mancini on his touchline words with David Moyes

"I've got other irons in the fire but I'm keeping them close to my chest."
John Bond trots out two cliches in one sentence after departing as manager

THE FUNNIEST MAN CITY QUOTES... EVER!

"Before we won the championship, I told the lads exactly how many goals we would score and how many points. I was exactly right. I'm brilliant!"
Malcolm Allison

"I took a knock – the bench here is very dangerous!"
Roberto Mancini whacked his head in the dugout

"It can only be stupid people who say I would sign players I did not know anything about."
Sven-Goran Eriksson

Can You Manage?

"We played extremely well with Beanie for the match against West Ham. He's come through our academy system, or rather my daughter's academy system, and he made the trip to Everton. Beanie got us a result today."
Stuart Pearce

"Watching City is probably the best laxative you can have."
Caretaker manager Phil Neal after a thrilling win over Bradford City

"A lot of hard work went into this defeat."
Malcolm Allison

THE FUNNIEST MAN CITY QUOTES... EVER!

"If you drive a Ferrari you can win, if you drive a Fiat Cinquecento, probably not."
Roberto Mancini on how to win the Champions League

"I may be able to put a good book tape on in the car on the way home and I will have a smile on my face."
Stuart Pearce is happy after City's win at Middlesbrough

"A coach who has worked in Argentina can work in any part of the world."
Manuel Pellegrini bigs himself up

Can You Manage?

"I want to get more players through the door while the window is open."
Mark Hughes

"I have seen the film The Alamo and right now I feel like I've got Davy Crockett behind me. Sometimes I feel like I could put my head in a bucket of water."
Stuart Pearce feels the heat after City are knocked out of the FA Cup by Blackburn

"I only shot three or four players in the dressing room."
Roberto Mancini

THE FUNNIEST MAN CITY QUOTES... EVER!

"The fans keep waiting for something to go wrong. I call it City-itis. It's a rare disease whose symptoms are relegation twice every three seasons."
Joe Royle

"I've served more time than Ronnie Biggs did for the Great Train Robbery."
Malcolm Allison on his touchline ban

"I like being manager. I like being angry every day."
Roberto Mancini

Can You Manage?

"I'm looking for a woman, but I keep landing on the same big old bloke."

Manager Stuart Pearce on leaping into the crowd for goal celebrations

Reporter: "Is the aim to win four trophies?"
Pep Guardiola: "What the f*ck? My happiness does not depend on if I am going to win all the titles or not. My target is now to be happy today, drink a little bit of wine, and tomorrow prepare for the [next] game. After we are going to see."

THE FUNNIEST MAN CITY QUOTES... EVER!

"I work here four or five months and I think when you build a house you don't start from the roof but the basement. We work very well, but we are near the roof."
Roberto Mancini on his building works

"I rang my secretary and said, 'What time do we kick off tonight?' And she said, 'Every 10 minutes'."
Alan Ball

"When you lose and the people say bullsh*t, that moment you are angry and you speak not properly, so that is how it is."
Pep Guardiola on dealing with the media

Can You Manage?

"You've never really been a manager until you've been sacked."

Brian Horton after taking over from Peter Reid as boss

"The plan is to get out of management while I've still got all my marbles and my hair."

Joe Royle

"It has been retired. It was gelded after last week. I had to knock its rocks off. It was not so much a lucky mascot any more. But my daughter, Chelsea, is glad to have him back."

Stuart Pearce gets rid of cuddly horse mascot Beanie after the 4-0 loss to Wigan

THE FUNNIEST MAN CITY QUOTES... EVER!

BOARDROOM BANTER

THE FUNNIEST MAN CITY QUOTES... EVER!

"I don't walk past him every day and ask if I've got his full support. But the other night he bought me a sandwich at the reserves' match and that's a real show of affection from our chairman."
Stuart Pearce on chairman John Wardle

"The problem? I can't drag the old boots on anymore and get out on the park and play. It would be a lot easier if I could."
New chairman Francis Lee

"I received my resignation by email."
Dennis Tueart after being removed as City director by new owner Thaksin Shinawatra

Boardroom Banter

"I've played in the World Cup, sweated out multi-million pound business deals, I've trained some good horses and I'm a father. But 90 minutes at Maine Road can make me feel like an old dish rag."
Francis Lee

"Peter Swales wore a wig, a blazer with an England badge on it and high-heeled shoes. As a man he really impressed me."
Malcolm Allison

"What other job is there where your entire livelihood depends on 11 daft lads?"
Francis Lee on football management

THE FUNNIEST MAN CITY QUOTES... EVER!

"Brian [Horton] will hear anything on his position from me first."

Francis Lee on his manager's status. "It's the first I've heard about it," added Horton after reading he was sacked in the paper

"The trouble was he had no repartee with the fans."

Peter Swales after firing Mel Machin

"If some other mug wants to take over, I'd be willing to walk out tomorrow."

Francis Lee feels the pressure

Boardroom Banter

"I see myself as a friendly advisor, not a dictator."

Francis Lee on claims he is meddling with the first team

"[Roberto] Mancini is lucky. He has an owner [Sheikh Mansour] who speaks little and asks only, 'What do you need?'"

Mario Balotelli

"I will still be coming to matches – mind you, I might have to wear a beard, dark glasses and a dirty raincoat."

Francis Lee after departing as chairman

THE FUNNIEST MAN CITY QUOTES... EVER!

BEST OF ENEMIES

THE FUNNIEST MAN CITY QUOTES... EVER!

"My celebration was directed at Gary Neville. He acted like a complete sock-sucker [boot-licker] when he said I wasn't worth £25m, just to suck up to the manager."
Carlos Tevez hits out at his old teammate after scoring a brace for City in their League Cup win over United

"If we win the derby, I'll jump off the stand roof with a parachute. Lose and I won't bother with the parachute."
Mike Summerbee on the Manchester derby in 2006

Best of Enemies

"If I have my way he will be out of the club. He just refused to go on. I don't know why. I cannot be happy with this situation. Would something like this happen at Bayern Munich, AC Milan or Manchester United?"

Roberto Mancini after Carlos Tevez appears to refuse to come on as a substitute against Bayern Munich

"I didn't feel right to play, so I didn't."

Carlos Tevez gives more detail on the fallout

"So then he tells me to keep on warming up and treats me like a dog."

Carlos Tevez explains further

THE FUNNIEST MAN CITY QUOTES... EVER!

"Too many people talk. Too many people speak about me bad. And now they need to shut up."
Mario Balotelli addresses his haters after City clinch the title

"My teammates were asking what I thought. And I wondered to myself: what's the moron talking about me for when I never said anything about him, when there was never any [issue] with us."
Carlos Tevez after Gary Neville had said the Argentine was not worth £25m

"Rooney's good but not the best in Manchester."
Mario Balotelli

Best of Enemies

"I don't think I'll ever get away from my reputation. If you tried googling me, you know I won't get away from it. If I ever do a book – which I won't – the title will be: Don't Google Me."
Craig Bellamy

"Last season, after a home game against Newcastle, we almost hit each other in the dressing room."
Carlos Tevez on Roberto Mancini

"I don't really know what was said, they were talking in Italian."
Joleon Lescott on an argument between Roberto Mancini and Carlos Tevez

THE FUNNIEST MAN CITY QUOTES... EVER!

"Google me and you will see I have been in this league for four or five years before going to Manchester City. Google me and see what I have done in this league. If I am not shooting enough, how am I going to score? I have put the ball into the net, how?"
Emmanuel Adebayor to Roberto Mancini after the manager said his scoring rate wasn't good enough

"He is a coach and he must give respect a little bit. He is always talking about everyone and that is not the correct way."
Yaya Toure tells Chelsea manager Jose Mourinho to keep quiet

Best of Enemies

"How I can say it without being rude?"

Samir Nasri fires back after Roberto Mancini criticises him

"Mancini said, 'You're an idiot and I don't know why I bought you'. I hate people who say 'Mario, you played well', then say to others, 'Mario was sh*t'. Roberto has never lied to me."

Mario Balotelli

"Hahahaha"

Edin Dzeko tweets after Manchester United lose 4-0 to MK Dons

THE FUNNIEST MAN CITY QUOTES... EVER!

"The club's owners ate a 100kg cake after winning the Premier League this season but when they and the players were all together, none of them shook his hand on his birthday. It shows they don't care about him. It's really sick."
Agent Dimitri Seluk says his client Yaya Toure was furious the club failed to wish him a happy 31st birthday

"Thanks for all the birthday messages today. Card from City just arrived... Must have got lost in the post. Haha. Jokes aside. Please do not take words that do not come out of MY mouth seriously. Judge my commitment to @MCFC by my performances."
Yaya Toure tweets

Best of Enemies

"We fought for an hour in the dressing room! I won because I don't have any scars."
Roberto Mancini on talk of a dust-up with Emmanuel Adebayor

"I know I get carried away by emotion. I have always been like that. I don't give a toss whether that pleases people or not."
Craig Bellamy

"[Roberto] Mancini and I had confrontations in every language. We have a love-hate relationship."
Carlos Tevez

THE FUNNIEST MAN CITY QUOTES... EVER!

"It seems [Alex] Ferguson is the president of England. Each time he speaks badly about a player, and he has said the worst about me, I never asked him to apologise. But if somebody makes a joke about him, you must apologise to him. But I don't apologise. There's no relationship at all between me and Ferguson."
Carlos Tevez

"They should celebrate their third-place achievement and I will focus on winning titles."
Samir Nasri takes a swipe at Arsenal fans after City win the Premier League

Best of Enemies

"I know what JT's like and nothing surprises me about him, so I'm not going to comment on that guy. I think everyone in football knows what the guy's like."

Craig Bellamy on John Terry, who had made the headlines after a bust-up with Wayne Bridge. Terry hit back: "People in glass houses should not throw stones"

"I sent my Christmas wishes to him, but he didn't answer. He's the world's best coach, but as a man he still has to learn manners and respect."

Mario Balotelli on Jose Mourinho

THE FUNNIEST MAN CITY QUOTES... EVER!

MANAGING PLAYERS

THE FUNNIEST MAN CITY QUOTES... EVER!

"I keep saying to him, 'France must have some really good defenders for you to not be in their team'. But the older ones will get older and he will get better."
Kevin Keegan on Sylvain Distin

"If you were a racehorse, they'd shoot you."
Francis Lee to the 37-year-old Mike Summerbee

"He's got lovely hair, I pull his hair all the time."
Stuart Pearce on Michael Essien tugging Bernardo Corradi's barnet

Managing Players

"Two days after a hamstring strain that would have kept anyone else out for a fortnight, on a freezing day when we were all training in bobble hats and gloves, he emerged, running out of the mist, wearing nothing but a pair of underpants and a towel wrapped round his head. That's why we call him Psycho."

Kevin Keegan on Stuart Pearce

"[Paulo] Wanchope took his goals well and he's a lovely big boy."

Joe Royle

THE FUNNIEST MAN CITY QUOTES... EVER!

"You sold yourself easier than a bloody prostitute."

Joe Mercer to Dave Bacuzzi who was given a torrid time by Cardiff's Ronnie Bird

"I would like to give him a punch because a player should play like this always."

Roberto Mancini after Samir Nasri's superb performance against Newcastle

"When [Gary] Flitcroft played for the A team, he had 'footballer' written all over his forehead."

Colin Bell

Managing Players

"When cars are designed, they feed the information into a computer and it throws out this aerodynamic design with the hatchback and all the trimmings. If you put the details for a centre half into a computer, especially a left-sided one, and you said he needs to be 6ft 3in, he needs to be quick, he needs to be strong, and he needs to be able to use the ball, then it would be Sylvain Distin."
Kevin Keegan

"He just needs to make his brain work. That is his only problem."
Roberto Mancini to Mario Balotelli

THE FUNNIEST MAN CITY QUOTES... EVER!

"If you created a template for the ideal striker to put into a computer, like they do with cars, and it then sends out the perfect aerodynamic hatchback, it would come out with Thierry Henry and Nicolas Anelka as the perfect strikers."

Kevin Keegan

"No, no, no. We can't have him. Isn't he the lad who threw a bed out of the window at Lilleshall?"

Joe Mercer is worried about signing Tony Coleman

Managing Players

"It feels as if I need my own special translator just for Mario [Balotelli]."
Roberto Mancini

"It won't be long before he has our supporters hanging from the rafters."
Alan Ball on new signing Georgi Kinkladze

"I am finished. We have six games and he will not play in the next six games."
Roberto Mancini is fed up with Mario Balotelli

THE FUNNIEST MAN CITY QUOTES... EVER!

"Joe Hart made a few mistakes around Christmas time and got crucified for them."
Joe Corrigan

"I'm pleased for Georgios [Samaras]. He can be a handful on any given day and trip over the ball on any given day."
Stuart Pearce

"As far as I'm concerned, Danny Tiatto doesn't exist."
Kevin Keegan blasts his player after getting sent off for a bad tackle against Blackburn

Managing Players

"I told Balotelli that if he played with me 10 years ago, I would have maybe punched him in the head on a daily basis. I don't speak with him every day, otherwise I would need a psychologist."
Roberto Mancini

"He couldn't – I do Thai kick-boxing."
Mario Balotelli hits back at Mancini

"Like the nightmare of a delirious parole officer."
Malcolm Allison on new buy Tony Coleman

THE FUNNIEST MAN CITY QUOTES... EVER!

"We are near Christmas, at the end of the year it is a very dangerous time for fireworks."

Roberto Mancini advises Mario Balotelli after his infamous firework incident

"There was one point where I am sure Richard Dunne thought he was Maradona."

Sven-Goran Eriksson on his skilful defender after City's FA Cup win over West Ham

"Mario needs two. And then after, you'll need another two."

Roberto Mancini when asked if Mario Balotelli needed a psychiatrist

Managing Players

"You're not a good player. In fact, you're a bad player. But I could make you into a fair player."
Malcolm Allison to Francis Lee

"Sergio [Aguero] is a photocopy of Romario."
Roberto Mancini

"Joe Hart should stay in goal and make saves. If anyone should criticise the team it should be me, not Joe Hart. I am the judge, not Joe Hart."
Roberto Mancini wants Joe Hart to stop criticising his own teammates

THE FUNNIEST MAN CITY QUOTES... EVER!

"Shaun Wright-Phillips has got a big heart. It's as big as him, which isn't very big, but it's bigger."

Kevin Keegan

"We want to ease Mario [Balotelli] back into action. He knew he would not play the full game. Sometimes in training when he misses a chance he holds his knee, and then when he scores, he doesn't!"

Roberto Mancini

Managing Players

"He didn't seem to grasp his own freakish strength. I said to him, 'You're a great header of the ball, you have a terrific shot, and you're the best, most powerful runner in the business. Every time you walk off the pitch unable to say you were streets ahead of the other 21 players, you have failed."
Malcolm Allison to Colin Bell

"He hasn't got a foul mouth in any way, shape or form – unlike his manager."
Stuart Pearce after Sylvain Distin was sent off at Chelsea for protesting

THE FUNNIEST MAN CITY QUOTES... EVER!

LIFESTYLE CHOICE

THE FUNNIEST MAN CITY QUOTES... EVER!

"Football and tits are mixed up in the tabloids. If a girl says, 'I am a footballer's girlfriend' they all think it's true. Anything goes and you cannot defend yourself."

Mario Balotelli

"I've raised the white flag with English food and when I refused a beer, my teammates looked at me as if I were an alien."

Rolando Bianchi

"My wife has been magic about it."

John Bond after news broke he had an affair with a club employee

Lifestyle Choice

"It is better they go with a woman than a drink. It is better. That is what I did when I was a player."
Roberto Mancini

"John Bond has blackened my name with his insinuations about the private lives of football managers. Both my wives are upset."
Malcolm Allison

"He's alright but he's getting some stick. It serves him right for having a flash car!"
Paul Dickov after Georgi Kinkladze's high-speed crash

THE FUNNIEST MAN CITY QUOTES... EVER!

Noel Gallagher: "Can we talk about music? I believe you're a Coldplay fan, is that right?"

Pep Guardiola: "And James Blunt."

Noel Gallagher: "That bit will never be on the TV."

Pep Guardiola: "I read an interview and read you don't like too much this guy..."

Noel Gallagher: "It's not that I don't like him, el Senor, it's that I hate him, that's all it is."

"I am focused on my football, my manager, girlfriends and my family."

Mario Balotelli

Lifestyle Choice

"I don't even leave my house. When my contract ends I will not return to Manchester ever – not even on holiday. There is nothing to do in Manchester. The weather, everything. It has nothing and the problem is I'm still speaking very poor English."
Carlos Tevez

"Life was f*cked. A lot of robbing, a difficult district. I had a very bad time. All the friends I had, I don't think any of them are at home. They're all in prison."
Sergio Aguero on growing up in Buenos Aires, Argentina

THE FUNNIEST MAN CITY QUOTES... EVER!

"When I was in my office after the [title-winning] game, Liam Gallagher from Oasis came in. He's a big fan of City and he planted a big kiss on my mouth – I didn't have time to react!"
Roberto Mancini

"Finally my little pig arrived! She is only 2 months old! Is a she but I called her SUPER! Actually can't find the willy so I think is a she, ahahaha, but maybe a he! Ahahah."
Mario Balotelli tweets

"You hear that rock music and it makes you want to throw yourself off a cliff."
Micah Richards

Lifestyle Choice

Head waiter: "Mr Allison, your bar bill – I have to tell you, it is enormous."

Malcolm Allison: "Is that all? You insult me. Don't come back until it's double that!"

"I struggled the first few days with breakfast. Instead of a croissant and cappuccino, I was faced with eggs."

Rolando Bianchi on adjusting to life in Manchester

"I have two or three of these in Serbia. John Deere tractors."

Aleksandar Kolarov's other car is a tractor

THE FUNNIEST MAN CITY QUOTES... EVER!

"The young players think that they have won something in football because they have two mobile phones and a house."

Carlos Tevez

"When I was at Inter Milan I had to call my mum to resolve every little problem. Here I have to deal with things on my own."

Mario Balotelli

"Did you know Alan Ball's missus used to come and watch us in training? One day she said to Keith Curle, 'You should have been tighter at the back'."

Nicky Summerbee

Lifestyle Choice

"I have started collecting press cuttings to make an album. Out of 100 things that are written about me, at most five are true."
Mario Balotelli

"My mother wanted me to be a folk dancer, so when my father went to Russia to work for three years, she hid away my football boots and took me to dancing classes."
Georgi Kinkladze

"Well I give up... dancing is definitely not my cup of tea, it's way easier to kick a ball lols!!"
Yaya Toure's random tweet

THE FUNNIEST MAN CITY QUOTES... EVER!

"I don't feel integrated into English life at all. We cannot speak English, we don't know the culture and we are scared of appearing rude. My two children are in nursery and I didn't realise we should take a cake for the rest of the class on their birthday. In China, we don't do things like that."

Sun Jihai on living in England

Policeman: "Why do you have £5,000 in your back pocket?"

Mario Balotelli: "Because I am rich."

Cops question and breathalyse the Italian after he crashed his car

Lifestyle Choice

"In my neighbourhood if you do that, you lose your legs or more, you don't survive."
Carlos Tevez reckons John Terry is lucky he doesn't live in Argentina after upsetting teammate Wayne Bridge

"There is great consolation in not playing and going home in a Porsche. In my day, the car park was all Vivas and Cortinas."
Joe Royle

"Take away Match of the Day and all the hangers-on and it's all very empty and lonely being a footballer."
Rodney Marsh

THE FUNNIEST MAN CITY QUOTES... EVER!

A FUNNY OLD GAME

THE FUNNIEST MAN CITY QUOTES... EVER!

"Second best is not good enough for this team. Although if someone turned around now and said, 'You will come second', I would take it."
Steve Howey

"Even if there is one game to go and we are 12 points behind, we'll still believe."
Joe Hart

"Join us in wishing @YayaToure a very happy 32nd birthday today!"
The club remembers to send a nice tweet the year after the midfielder got upset

A Funny Old Game

"Coming to Manchester City, if anything, is more exciting than being at Real Madrid."
Steve McManaman

"Need a rest? If I need a rest I'll sleep on the team bus on the way to the game."
Nigel de Jong

"Pleased to meet you Ma'am. Give my love to your mum and dad."
Tony Coleman to Princess Anne before the 1969 FA Cup Final. The Queen later sent a telegram thanking him for his best wishes

THE FUNNIEST MAN CITY QUOTES... EVER!

"I never understood the intention of that poster. What was the point? Tell me. Was it to welcome me to Manchester City, or was it to anger Manchester United? Nobody ever told me."

Carlos Tevez on the famous 'Welcome to Manchester' poster

"F*cking hell, I just can't believe it. It's a brilliant experience."

Micah Richards curses in a live TV interview after scoring in City's FA Cup tie at Aston Villa, in 2006

A Funny Old Game

"She told me off a little bit for it and said I was making myself look bad on TV."
Micah Richards was later ticked off by his mum

"I can't sign Rangers geez. I can't. No chance."
Craig Bellamy, who had previously played for Celtic, refuses to put his name on a Rangers shirt for a fan at Glasgow airport

Reporter: "How do City plan to deal with Eden Hazard?"
Vincent Kompany: "You'd almost hope that Eden Hazard would have diarrhoea."

THE FUNNIEST MAN CITY QUOTES... EVER!

"Angels don't win you anything except a place in heaven. Football teams need one or two vagabonds."

Billy McNeill

"Goalkeepers aren't born today until they are in their 30s."

Kevin Keegan

"The pitch was playable. I've been in football over 25 years and it has become a game for poofters."

John Burridge after City's game was postponed

A Funny Old Game

"If someone throws a banana at me in the street, I will go to prison because I will kill him."
Mario Balotelli on potential racism issues at Euro 2012, in Ukraine and Poland

"I want to stay in football. What else can I do? I do media and that farting around, but there's no passion there. Who wants to sit and commentate on Middlesbrough v Everton? Where's the job satisfaction in that?"
Stuart Pearce closing in on retirement

"Balotelli costs as much as the Mona Lisa."
Mario Balotelli's agent Mino Raiola

THE FUNNIEST MAN CITY QUOTES... EVER!

"I remember a big fat red-haired bloke who used to torture us at the start of every season when it was boiling hot. He would lean over the wall with his fat stomach showing and a bottle of beer in his hand and leer at us shouting, 'You're not fit!'"

Francis Lee remembers a particular Man City supporter

"I'll have to see whether any of [Roy] Keane's studs are still in there."

Alf-Inge Haaland before undergoing a knee scan

A Funny Old Game

"It is not as if you are doing your homework and a fly comes into the room. There is a ball. That is it."

Joe Hart responds to critics who claim he lacks the necessary concentration levels

"Dribbling and leaving your opponent on his backside is what life is for."

Sergio Aguero

"You won't get me flicking on a [football] phone-in. I'd rather listen to a game of chess on the radio. Phone-ins are platforms for idiots."

Joe Royle

THE FUNNIEST MAN CITY QUOTES... EVER!

"A lot of people in football don't have much time for the press, they say they are amateurs. But I say, 'Noah built the Ark, but the Titanic was built by professionals'."
Malcolm Allison

"When I saw Owen score that goal for England against Argentina in 1998 I thought, 'You little sh*t!' Even aged 10, I knew they couldn't allow him that much space."
Sergio Aguero on Michael Owen

A Funny Old Game

"England did nothing in the World Cup, so why are they bringing books out? 'We got beat in the quarter-finals, we played like sh*t, here's my book'. Who wants to read that? I don't."
Joey Barton on the autobiographies released by England players

"I had 15 messages after the game. The best one was from my mum which said, 'Come outside and get some sweets!'."
Nedum Onuoha after receiving racist abuse from Serbian fans during an England U21 fixture

THE FUNNIEST MAN CITY QUOTES... EVER!

"I still have the original Superman pants... I have upgraded them so they will make an appearance when it's the right moment – and the new ones are much, much better!"

Stephen Ireland on his goal-celebration prop

"At the start of the season anyone could have gone in goal for us – it didn't require any ability to be in goal."

Joe Hart

"There's no loyalty in football any more."

Craig Bellamy after leaving his eighth club Man City for Cardiff

A Funny Old Game

"I could have been buried somewhere. I love scoring goals, but whatever I do now, I say, 'Yes, you are scoring goals, but you could be in a coffin now, you could be in paradise'. I don't know, it's very hard."

Emmanuel Adebayor on surviving the gun attack on the Togo football team at the African Cup of Nations, in Angola

"Look at the fans, they're f*cking... They've been there since day one. I can't believe it, it's unbelievable."

Micah Richards (for the second time) swears in a live pitchside TV interview after the FA Cup final, in 2011

THE FUNNIEST MAN CITY QUOTES... EVER!

"It's not just about money but where the club wants to go and where Joey wants to go... If City had come back with the offer we asked for, then he would have signed the contract."
Joey Barton's agent Willie McKay claims it's not about money... then says there wasn't enough money

"That statement was completely bizarre."
Stuart Pearce responds to McKay

"Manchester is our city. This is our city and it's not their city. It's a massive city and it can take two massive clubs and that's what it's got."
Kevin Keegan

A Funny Old Game

"I remember a game against Liverpool. I was stood on one leg hooking the ball with the other. Next thing, Tommy Smith took my standing leg away and I finished in a heap. 'Never stand on one leg when I'm around', growled Tommy."
Mike Summerbee

"It's not easy to win 5-0 at home against a Premier League team but we did. Was it 6-0? Oh!"
Edin Dzeko loses count of how many goals City scored past West Ham in the League Cup

THE FUNNIEST MAN CITY QUOTES... EVER!

CALL THE MANAGER

THE FUNNIEST MAN CITY QUOTES... EVER!

"I have watched Barnsley and it is clear they are not Real Madrid."
Roberto Mancini on Man City's cup tie against the Championship outfit

"I saw the celebration. Superman – super goal."
Sven-Goran Eriksson on Stephen Ireland baring his Superman pants after netting against Sunderland

"I went over to see Robbie [Fowler] in Liverpool, risked getting my tyres and wheels nicked to speak to him."
Kevin Keegan on trying to sign the striker

Call the Manager

"You lucky old b*stards! What a way to earn a living."
Joe Mercer to the City players in 1968

"To score four goals when you are playing like pigs in labour is fantastic."
Joe Royle after Man City's 4-1 win against Blackburn

"If I had played today I would have scored two or three goals."
Roberto Mancini fancies putting his boots on again

THE FUNNIEST MAN CITY QUOTES... EVER!

"Not many teams will come to Arsenal and get anything, home or away."
Kevin Keegan

"It is better that we don't talk about this."
Roberto Mancini on a mysterious Sergio Aguero injury

"He wears a suit, so he's a tactician. He wears a tracksuit, so he's a motivator. He carries a clipboard, so he's a bus conductor."
Stuart Pearce on the many talents of Rafa Benitez

Call the Manager

"I can't believe what I've seen tonight. It was a disgrace. If we'd have scored another goal in that atmosphere I don't think we would have got out alive."
Joe Royle after City's trip to Millwall

"I'm not sure if it's a good draw or not – I love Newcastle United Football Club and I'm getting to love Manchester City."
Kevin Keegan after his City team are drawn against Newcastle in the FA Cup

"Keith Curle has an ankle injury but we'll have to take it on the chin."
Alan Ball

THE FUNNIEST MAN CITY QUOTES... EVER!

Reporter: "Stan Collymore said you are going back to Spain with your tail between your legs. What do you think about these comments?"

Pep Guardiola: [Looks bewildered] "Stan Collymore?"

"My biggest concern is that I've got two great individuals who are masters of their trade, yet there is still work to be done with them."
Kevin Keegan

"We'll call the police."
Roberto Mancini when asked how City could stop Cristiano Ronaldo

Call the Manager

"It is a very strange goal because the ball changed direction. Two balloons made a one-two with Michael Ball. I have never seen a goal like that."
Sven-Goran Eriksson on Sheffield United's opening goal which went in with the help of balloons in the penalty area

"After their goal I felt squeaky-bum time!"
Roberto Mancini uses Sir Alex Ferguson's famous line after title-chasing City went a goal down against Chelsea

THE FUNNIEST MAN CITY QUOTES... EVER!

"Glenn [Roeder] is going to bring a couple of sumo costumes down so we might have a dust-up in the technical area, that should make good TV."

Stuart Pearce refers to the Arsene Wenger-Alan Pardew bust-up ahead of City's match with Newcastle

"At half-time, I walked off and said to Derek Fazackerley, 'Where's the nearest job centre?'"

Kevin Keegan on City's amazing recovery to come back from 3-0 down, with 10 men, to beat Tottenham 4-3

Call the Manager

"We will win the European Cup. European football is full of cowards and we'll terrorise them."
Malcolm Allison

"It was awful. Sometimes you have one or two players who are not doing their job, but on this occasion we had about a dozen."
Sven-Goran Eriksson is so upset he loses count of players in a team

"I personally will always have a soft spot for Willie."
Kevin Keegan is disappointed with the departure of coach Willie Donachie

THE FUNNIEST MAN CITY QUOTES... EVER!

"In the dressing room at the interval, I told the lads that we'd be playing for pride and that I'd be praying for a miracle."
Kevin Keegan on what proved to be an inspired half-time team talk as City fought back from 3-0 down to beat Spurs 4-3 with 10 men

"I've told the players that people will still be watching that match when we're all six feet under... or cremated... or whatever we intend to do with ourselves."
Kevin Keegan is thrilled after that amazing Spurs victory

Call the Manager

"We had to dig in and get back into the game. But we'll look back on this game and performance as three points lost."

Mark Hughes forgets you get a point for a draw after being held by Newcastle

"I personally feel that Millwall, along with Wolves, are the best side in this division. Apart from us."

Kevin Keegan

"We'll be the first team to play on Mars!"

Malcolm Allison

THE FUNNIEST MAN CITY QUOTES... EVER!

"I think the league table is a pretty good barometer of how you are doing."
Kevin Keegan

"We have signed two young players, although one is younger than the other."
Sven-Goran Eriksson

"The goal of the month has been disallowed... I can't remember seeing such a goal disallowed – not even in Roy of the Rovers."
Joe Royle on Danny Tiatto's ruled-out strike against Middlesbrough

Call the Manager

"He can't head it! He can't pass it! He's no good on his left foot!"

Malcolm Allison tries to put off suitors interested in future star Colin Bell playing for Bury as City prepare a bid

"He and I did not speak the same language – and I do not mean Italian, Spanish or English."

Roberto Mancini is not a fan of City chief executive Ferran Soriano

"We haven't got the distraction of the Champions League or the European Cup, like some teams have."

Kevin Keegan

THE FUNNIEST MAN CITY QUOTES... EVER!

TALKING BALLS

THE FUNNIEST MAN CITY QUOTES... EVER!

"They treat me like Maradona over here. I hope I can repay all this love on the field. I just can't score any goals by hand."

Robinho

"I kicked a few full-backs in my time but I always sent them flowers afterwards."

Mike Summerbee

"The sooner [Steve] McMahon returns the better. I have been so stiff recently on the morning after matches that I thought rigor mortis had set in."

Peter Reid

Talking Balls

"When I decide to score, I score. I think I am a genius. I believe I am more intelligent than the average person. If you find another guy like me, I'll buy you dinner. The talent God gave me is beautiful, magnificent, but it's difficult to deal with because people are always ready to judge you. Only a few people have such talent, so only a few people should be able to judge what I am doing."
Mario Balotelli

"If I achieve what I want to then I'll mark a distinct era in football. I'm the Che Guevara of modern soccer."
Sergio Aguero

THE FUNNIEST MAN CITY QUOTES... EVER!

Robinho: "Chelsea made me a great proposal and I accepted."

Reporter: "You mean Manchester City, right?"

Robinho: "Yeah, Manchester. Sorry!"

City's new signing is unveiled at a press conference

"I'd rather have a slim [Carlos] Tevez than one with a belly."

Nigel de Jong

"My wife always said, 'You love Malcolm Allison more than you love me'."

Mike Summerbee

Talking Balls

"I am not crazy, absolutely not, although sometimes I do strange things that are considered entertaining."
Mario Balotelli

Sir Alf Ramsay: "I'll be watching you for the first 45 minutes and if you don't work harder, I'll pull you off at half-time."
Rodney Marsh: "Blimey – at Manchester City, all we get is an orange and a cup of tea."

"[Milan owner] Silvio Berlusconi said that [Antonio] Cassano is the best Italian talent. He is either wrong or he doesn't know Balotelli."
Mario Balotelli

THE FUNNIEST MAN CITY QUOTES... EVER!

"There's only one that is a little stronger than me: Messi. All the others are behind me."
Mario Balotelli doesn't lack belief

Q: "Do your mates look like other Scooby-Doo characters?"
A: "Yeah, the wife looks like Daphne. One of my mates looks like Thelma... nah, not really. It's just me with the uncanny resemblance. To the dog, I think."
Steve McManaman

"I am already a God and I didn't do anything!"
Robinho enjoys the adulation at City

Talking Balls

"People said that I must have kept all the bricks that came through my window and put a snooker room on the side of my house. I did keep the bricks but I built a five-bedroom detached house in Wimslow with them."
Steve Daley on being ridiculed by fans after his British record transfer failed to work out

"Somebody would give him the ball and I'd make a run to collect it in the box and it would never arrive. I'd turn around and he'd be juggling it like a bloody seal."
Neil Young on Rodney Marsh

THE FUNNIEST MAN CITY QUOTES... EVER!

"They think he's just some hooligan from up north. He is anything but. He's a gentleman."
Joe Hart on Andy Carroll

"There are two Marios. There is one who turns up sometimes in training and it is a bit cold and he is not too interested. The other time he really wants it."
James Milner on Mario Balotelli's split personality

"If I'm flying around like Clark Kent in goals, I still won't play on Saturday."
Frustrated goalkeeper Shay Given

Talking Balls

"When I score, I don't celebrate because it's my job. When a postman delivers letters, does he celebrate?"

Mario Balotelli

"It's just like playing alongside Barbara Streisand."

Mike Summerbee on Rodney Marsh

"He sees you when you can't even see yourself."

Paulo Wanchope on Ali Benarbia's passing skills

THE FUNNIEST MAN CITY QUOTES... EVER!

"We've got all kinds of nationalities at Maine Road, but most of the lads think my accent is a bit strange as well."
Steve Howey

"Why always me?"
Mario Balotelli's t-shirt

"Tony [Book] was a bricklayer as well as playing hundreds of games for Bath City before joining us in his 30s. No wonder he played with such enthusiasm."
Mike Summerbee

Talking Balls

"He is one of those players – and I don't think he will be unhappy with me saying it – that some days you look at him in training and he is useless."

Joe Hart on Sergio Aguero

"All my season was sh*t. Can I say that? It was not very good, today maybe I play more for the team."

Mario Balotelli's rhetorical question in a live TV interview after City's 2011 FA Cup Final victory

THE FUNNIEST MAN CITY QUOTES... EVER!

"I do miss Mario Balotelli, actually. He was crazy, he liked to be the centre of attention and it was like having a 12-year-old in the dressing room at times. You had to keep him busy. We did a Christmas event for some children at the ground, and Mario had to wait about half-an-hour to do his bit. We were thinking, 'What can we do with him? He's going to be an absolute nightmare'. He ended up sitting in on an interview with Joe Hart for 20 minutes! Then someone gave him an iPad to play Angry Birds on."
James Milner

"From time to time, I'm a jerk."
Samir Nasri

Talking Balls

"It was awesome. I was watching it. Brilliant. The gaffer was training and Stefan properly did him."

Joe Hart enjoyed watching Stefan Savic tackle boss Roberto Mancini

"I should walk away, but I can't sometimes."

Andy Morrison on holding his temper

Journalist: "Have you received this sort of adulation before?"

Ali Benarbia: "It happens at every club I play for!"

THE FUNNIEST MAN CITY QUOTES... EVER!

"I'm getting to that age where I'm not 18 anymore."

Micah Richards, aged 26

"I didn't cry. I just told him that I would like to leave."

Robinho to Real Madrid president Ramon Calderon

"It's not every day an athlete is nicknamed after a cartoon character!"

Sergio Aguero on his likeness to 'Kun' in a Japanese cartoon

Talking Balls

"I'm not a bad guy but I'm shy; it's difficult to be here giving an interview."
Mario Balotelli

"There were a few tweets about Asda, so I was asking the masseurs where they shopped. I don't shop in Asda... I've never got close enough to actually accuse anyone of running it. I thought I had [with the masseurs], but I realised they didn't have enough banter!"
James Milner is trying to track down the owners of the @BoringMilner parody Twitter account

THE FUNNIEST MAN CITY QUOTES... EVER!

"We were playing five-a-side and we were losing because he [Mario Balotelli] didn't work, which is evident. He swore at me in Italian and he thought I didn't understand. But I know a bit of Italian lingo so I said, 'Who are you talking to?' He said it again, so we squared up and I offered him out, but he said no."
Micah Richards on a training pitch row with Mario Balotelli

"It's hilarious sometimes. Even when he is angry in a match, all you get from him is 'ruddy hell' or 'flipping heck'."
Joe Corrigan on Colin Bell

Talking Balls

Yaya Toure: "Me and [David Silva] will have an arm wrestle to settle who scored the first goal!! Hope you guys enjoyed my second!"

David Silva: "Yaya Toure, the goal is mine, thanks for the assist, I will assist you hopefully many times during the season!!!!"

Yaya Toure: "Looks like someone has stolen my friend [David Silva's] phone... Or he's just got very brave!"

David Silva: "Wrong my friend, I have my phone and you know I will take you on anytime Yaya Toure."

Twitter banter between the teammates over who is claiming the second goal in the 3-0 win over West Brom

THE FUNNIEST MAN CITY QUOTES... EVER!

"For him, his players' sexual activity must take place before midnight in order to get a good night's sleep – even if they are free tomorrow. He [Pep Guardiola] said that he placed this rule on Messi and his muscles improved since."
Samir Nasri on Pep Guardiola's sex ban for the City squad

"It can't be Sunday every day. There are also Mondays and Tuesdays."
George Weah

Talking Balls

Reporter: "What have you learnt from David Seaman?"

David James: "Hair grows fast."

"What's his name? Wil... ? No, I don't know him, but the next time I play against Arsenal, I will keep a close eye on him."

Mario Balotelli finishes ahead of Jack Wilshere to win the Golden Boy trophy – and then claims he'd never heard of the Gunners midfielder

THE FUNNIEST MAN CITY QUOTES... EVER!

"I know I've been out for quite long… but still #ChrikSamara."

Bacary Sagna's response on social media after Chris Kamara mistakenly calls him 'Sacary Bagna' on air

"The internet is cut off. The dressing room is on the bottom floor, three floors down. There isn't even 3G connection there. We are incommunicado there."

Pablo Zabaleta says Pep Guardiola has switched off the players' Wi-Fi at the club's training ground

Talking Balls

"Maybe it's a fault in my make-up, but I can assure the fans I'm not devoid of feeling."
Colin Bell

"I'd only look as fast as Ryan Giggs if you stuck me in the 1958 FA Cup Final."
Rick Holden

"I'm not more famous than Tintin. I don't think I'll ever top him."
Vincent Kompany on being a Belgian icon

THE FUNNIEST MAN CITY QUOTES... EVER!

REFFING HELL

THE FUNNIEST MAN CITY QUOTES... EVER!

"How can women referees make accurate decisions if they have never been tackled from behind by a 14-stone centre half, elbowed in the ribs, or even caught offside?"
Joe Royle

"I asked the fourth official if it was a yellow card because I thought the referee had forgotten his yellow cards in the dressing room."
Roberto Mancini was not happy with a bad challenge on Gareth Barry

Reffing Hell

"Next thing we'll be giving our handbags to the linesmen before we skip on to the field."
Mike Summerbee on football getting too soft

"Don't talk about the game, talk about Uriah Rennie – that's what he likes and he's always been the same."
Kevin Keegan

"I've had a player sent off for aggressive walking! I think I must have missed a rule change somewhere."
Joe Royle after Kevin Horlock was shown a red card

THE FUNNIEST MAN CITY QUOTES... EVER!

"The referee, he ate too much for Christmas. He was not in good form."
Roberto Mancini is angry with referee Kevin Friend after City lost at Sunderland

"I thought Michael Johnson should have had a penalty but the referee booked him for filming."
Sven-Goran Eriksson

"It's like a toaster, the ref's shirt pocket. Every time there's a tackle, up pops a yellow card."
Kevin Keegan

Reffing Hell

"I have to admit that what I said to the referee outside his room afterwards was out of order. That was wrong and I owe him a letter of apology for that."

Kevin Keegan apologises to referee Steve Dunn for branding him a "homer" after losing away at Newcastle

"We asked the fourth official to tell the referee to stop the game and take away the balloons – or kill them."

Sven-Goran Eriksson gets serious

THE FUNNIEST MAN CITY QUOTES... EVER!

SAY THAT AGAIN?

THE FUNNIEST MAN CITY QUOTES... EVER!

"Football injuries happen unfortunately and if it happens, it happens."

James Milner

"We miss Maine Road but we don't really miss it."

Kevin Keegan

"I'm not a believer in luck, but I do believe you need it."

Alan Ball

"Nicolas Anelka left Arsenal for £23million and they built a training ground on him."

Kevin Keegan

Say That Again?

"Maybe we were unlucky today but some time in the season we will have unluck, as you say."
Sven-Goran Eriksson after City overcame Man United

"This is a difficult division. Apart from the top four, it's dog eat dog, and we have just eaten one of the dogs."
Kevin Keegan after City's win over Bolton

"We haven't been good consistently. We're consistent but inconsistent. Inconsistently consistent."
David James

THE FUNNIEST MAN CITY QUOTES... EVER!

"Life wouldn't be worth living if you could buy confidence, because the rich people would have it all and everybody else would... would, well, have to make their own arrangements."
Kevin Keegan

"I was still, you know, throwing my clothes out of the pram a little bit."
Joey Barton on his 2005 transfer request

"The under-17s are doing very well. You get bunches of players like you do bananas, though that is a bad comparison."
Kevin Keegan

Say That Again?

"Danny Tiatto is not going to make a mistake on purpose."
Kevin Keegan

"The best way to win games is to score goals."
Manuel Pellegrini

"All three games are equally as important and we need to concentrate on all of them the same."
James Milner

"Some of our defending was indefensible."
Mark Hughes

THE FUNNIEST MAN CITY QUOTES... EVER!

"The manager picks the best team he thinks will win the game."
James Milner

"I can't promise anything, but I promise 100 per cent."
Paul Power

"At the time it happened, I regretted it in hindsight."
Joey Barton

"The tide is very much in our court now."
Kevin Keegan

Say That Again?

"My mum always told me not to go near the main road."
Kevin Keegan during his first press conference at Manchester City

"I have to speak to the players. Hug them, kick their arse!"
Pep Guardiola

"People will say that was typical City, which really annoys me. But that's typical City, I suppose."
Kevin Keegan

THE FUNNIEST MAN CITY QUOTES... EVER!

www.ingramcontent.com/pod-product-compliance
Lightning Source LLC
Chambersburg PA
CBHW050253120526
44590CB00016B/2327